W9-BNC-947

CREATION
OR
EVOLUTION

WHAT IS
THE
TRUTH?

W.J. OUWENEEL

ISBN 0-88172-145-X

Publishers of Select Christian Literature. . . A Nonprofit Corporation

BELIEVERS **BOOKSHELF, Inc.**

P. O. Box 261   Sunbury, Pennsylvania 17801

P. O. Box 242 ● Niagara-on-the-Lake
Ontario, Canada L0S 1J0

Cover design by Landgraff Associates
Toronto, Ontario, Canada.

Printed in U.S.A.

TABLE OF CONTENTS

FOREWORD
to the Second English Edition

The previous edition of this booklet has been well received among Christians in many countries. Originally published in the Netherlands, it first appeared in English in 1976. Here we would like to repeat some remarks made by the author in the foreword to the second Dutch edition:

"This booklet was written especially for young people. Some older perons considered the booklet to be 'childish' — indeed, that can happen to booklets that are written for youngsters.

A biology teacher thought the booklet to be 'unscientific', which is something I gladly admit. But he himself, I imagine, simplifies his subject to reach the students he is teaching.

More serious is the fact that some have called the booklet 'unchristian,' because of my attitude toward certain theories that undermine the Scriptures. I fear that such remarks are prompted by the same spirit that will cause many 'Christians' to be 'nice' to the antichrist when he comes."

He also expressed that he had made efforts to minimize remarks that might have seemed sarcastic.

"However under present circumstances I am unfortunately obliged to alert the students to the fact that teachers, in spite of their firm assertions, are not always right. I merely observe that most of them (just as many of my colleagues in research) are simply not well informed of the arguments against the belief in evolutionism and similar beliefs. Yet many . . . have been lulled asleep by it.

Again I have been disturbed by the rather naive reactions many had to this booklet, they cried triumphantly: 'Oh, but I don't have a problem at all, I believe in creation AND evolution!' That is why I have elaborated a little more on this point too."

We hope with the author that this booklet may be of help to many Christians, especially Christian students. May the Lord bless it to this end.

The Translator
Ajax, Canada, May 1982

Chapter One

Hook, Line and Sinker

This booklet is written especially for young people who today face a difficult problem. "What, actually, is the truth? Was the world *created* by God or has it come about by *evolution*?"

That is indeed a most important question! Perhaps you had been taught in your family that all things were created by God and you had accepted the Biblical story as truth. Then at school, from your teachers (or perhaps even during religious instructions!), you heard a different story! There you were told that the earth developed very slowly from a "gas nebula" or something of the sort. And the plants and animals also were not created but came into being by themselves, spontaneously, out of dead matter. First, so it was claimed, there were infintesimal, extremely simple "organisms", and from these developed, *very* gradually, larger and more complicated organisms (that is, plants and animals). This took millions of years, so they told you! And men? They developed very slowly from some kind of ape-like mammal. And that took many hundreds of thousands of years as well.

There you have the dilemma! What is the truth —
Creation or Evolution? Or on a more personal note:
Are you an improved version of some ape or are you
a creature made by God? Perhaps you respond: "Wait
a minute, my teacher (or minister) says that creation
and evolution are not at all two opposing ideas! He
says that it is very well possible that God created by
means of evolution. In that case God would have
'created' the plants and the animals by allowing them
to develop gradually from one form into another. . ."

Well yes, God *could* have done that. But did God
do so? Does your teacher think this because the Bible
says that God created in that manner? Not at all. He
is very well aware that "creation" in the Bible is presented as a sudden act of God. In the Psalms we read,
"For He (God) spoke, and it was done; He comman-
ded, and it stood fast" (Psalm 33:9). Your teacher
knows very well that the Bible does not speak at all
of periods of millions of years in which God gradually
formed the plants, animals and men. The Bible says
rather, "in *six days* the Lord made the heavens and
earth, the sea, and all that is in them, and rested the
seventh day" (Exodus 20:11).

Your teacher or minister may speak about a God
who creates by means of evolution, but he has no
support from God's Word! The Bible does not speak
of a slow development over millions of years, but of
sudden acts of creation during one week of six days.
The problem is therefore: either creation as the Bible
speaks of it, *or* evolution.

But how can it be explained that your teacher con-
fesses to be a Christian (he or she speaks about a God
Who creates), and yet believes in evolution although
he knows that it conflicts with the simple teaching of
the Bible? It is because he has been taught that evolution is an irrefutable, scientific fact which no sen-

sible scientist questions! And so he concludes that the literal meaning of the Bible cannot be true, and he finally gives a twist to it by declaring that God created by means of evolution; he supposes that so-called *theistic evolution* solves all his problems.

But by doing this your teacher alienates himself from both groups with which he is attempting to align himself. If he tells his unbelieving colleagues that he believes in evolution, that he is really not *that* old-fashioned, but that he believes that God directed the evolutionary process, they just laugh at him. The real confirmed evolutionists do not need God; there is no room for God in their teaching. They say: "Give us millions and billions of years, and blind chance will do the rest." *Time* and *chance* are the gods that beget evolution.

And if your teacher turns to his Bible-believing fellow Christians and tells them that he also believes in creation, that he is not *that* unchristian, but that he believes that God created by means of evolution, they look at him with pity. The faithful Christians who dare to take God at His Word, know very well that your teacher understands by "creation" something entirely different than the Bible. There is no room for evolution in their faith.

Just imagine what kind of god is required to satisfy his theistic evolutionary belief. As his highest creative work this god must have had man in view but it took him billions of years to evolve man. Moreover, he supposedly developed man by way of death, destruction and survival of the fittest in a struggle for life. He is supposed to have followed a plan that produced thousands of failures and blind sidepaths as well as thousands of "unsuccessful" species which he discarded, until finally, by trial and error, his goal ("man") was reached. Is this the God of the Bible?

In spite of the efforts of many Christian teachers to press this idea of theistic evolution upon their pupils, the problem looms as large as ever: "What is the truth — Creation or Evolution?" Both cannot simultaneously be true. It appears that you are being asked to swallow one of two ideas, hook, line and sinker.

Either:

A — God made the world in six days, as you have heard and were taught since you were very little,

or:

B — man evolved, as your teacher (and perhaps even your minister) affirms, and they try to base this on the argument that all scientific people now believe in evolution because it has been scientifically proven.

The choice appears to boil down to whether we must accept and believe what some claim to be a hopelessly out-dated religious book, or hyper-modern science!

What must you believe: an evolutionary theory, thought out by men, but not supported by facts, or the Bible, the perfect Word that comes directly from the Creator?

What is the truth — Creation or Evolution?

Chapter Two

Cock and Bull Stories

I am afraid that nowadays most biology teachers — whether they are called Christians or not — tell their pupils that evolution is a scientific fact, accepted by every scientist. But you better not conclude that those teachers are simply trying to deceive their pupils: of course they are not. They really *believe* that evolution is a genuine fact. But they have not examined the facts for themselves, for unfortunately most biologists have never made a thorough study of the so-called proofs of the existence of evolution! That may sound strange, but it is true. Evolution happens to be a very specialized subject that only a small proportion of the biologists have studied thoroughly.

How then do the biology teachers "know" so positively that they are descendents from the simplest organisms by process of evolution? Well, they believe it on the authority of others. They have learned to accept evolution as a scientific fact without having thoroughly studied the "proofs." Moreover, they have never yet met a biologist who had another opinion.

It may seem strange but yet it is true that the less someone understands evolution, the more he believes in it! Fortunately, many who specialize in evolution are careful, critical investigators. But their disciples who have only *heard* about it and who have never seen the complicated problems connected with belief in evolution, have no difficulty in accepting it, and they become antagonistic when someone raises an objection. The funniest (or rather the saddest) part is that, apparently, many ministers and theologians, who have absolutely no knowledge of biology, are becoming the most enthusiastic defenders of belief in evolution. Poor church people!

Yes, and the teenage highschool students who understand the problems even less than the students of biology, also become fiery defenders. For a time I was a teacher of biology in a Christian school and, would you believe it, the students were trying to talk *me* into believing evolution! Their teacher in the elementary school (who naturally was quite ignorant on the subject of evolution) together with their instructor in religion (who only repeated some things he had heard about evolution) had so poisoned the minds of these youngsters that they looked at me in unbelief and pity when I told them that I, a scientist, did not believe the fairy tales that they had learned.

Now let us see if everything about evolution is true that your teacher, in all sincerity, has dished up.

He may have told you, "No sensible biologist doubts the truth of evolution."

That is a real cock and bull story. He may believe it to be true, but it is not, as we will see. I for one do not believe in it, although I have made an intensive study of the so-called "proofs." In addition I have done research in the two biological fields that have provided the most powerful "proofs" of evolution, namely embryology (the study of the development of unborn organisms) and genetics (the study of heredity).

I am not the only doubter! For some years now I have been a member of the Creation Research Society (CRS). To become a member one must be a graduate scientist, believe in creation as the Bible tells it and reject evolution. The CRS consists of more than five hundred scientists, among whom are biologists, geologists, chemists, physicists, doctors and professors. I have met quite a few of them and I can assure you that they are to a man "sensible" people who have their wits about them! Some of them, such as Professor John N. Moore of the University of Michigan, have won great fame in their own scientific field.

Please, never again let anyone try to tell you that *all* scientists believe in evolution. In many countries you can find scores of scientists that do not believe in it. Just take a look at history. Have you heard in school of Faraday, of Maxwell, of Lord Kelvin, of Louis Pasteur? All of these were very famous scholars, but they were also confirmed "creationists" (people who believed in creation) and they vigorously opposed the rising evolutionism of Lamarck and Darwin.

The second cock and bull story often dished up at school is: "Evolution is a scientific fact." This again is done in good faith (at least, let us hope it is) although anyone who reflects a little should sense that he can never say that. It just isn't that simple to establish the "facts," to separate fact from fiction. Is it a fact that the sun shines? Yes, of course; if we doubt that we might as well finish with science, because then we could not trust our own senses any longer.

13

Is it also a fact that there is a change of seasons? Yes, surely, for in the first place that change is still taking place so that we can observe it all around us, and in the second place we know from our own memory and from the history books that this change of seasons has always taken place.

Is it also a fact that there was a Battle of Waterloo? That is more difficult, for that battle is no longer continuing and there are no people alive today who took part in that battle. Here our senses do not help us any longer. And yet we believe that there was such a battle because we have sufficient confidence in the historical sources of that period. But is it also a fact that there was a war between the Greeks and the Trojans as described by the Greek poet Homer? Ah, that is still more difficult, for we have not as much confidence in the historical accuracy of Homer's description. Some say, "There was such a war, but Homer and his contemporaries have embellished it with a great deal of fantasy." Others assert, "No, there never was such a war; the whole affair is a fiction of Greek imagination."

What can we learn from this? Well, that the question whether to regard a particular historical event (and evolution is just that!) as fact or fiction depends on the question: How trustworthy are my historical sources? If someone supposes that this historical process still takes place today, then I obviously pose the second question: Can I still observe this process around me today? And so it is with evolution. Of course, by far the greater part of the supposed evolution took place when no people existed. Consequently no one was present to give us an eye-witness account of it. We possess, therefore, no written evidence. But we have other historical sources — the strata and the fossils found in them. You know of course, that the earth's crust consists of different lay-

14

ers, formed one after the other, and that the fossils in them are the petrified remains of plants and animals. The two important questions are therefore:

1. Do the strata and the fossils furnish evidence that some time in the past an evolution took place from lower to higher organisms?

2. Does nature at the present time furnish evidence that *today* a similar evolution is taking place, and does it indicate *how* that evolutionary process is carried on?

The evolutionists answer these questions with a hearty "yes" and conclude: evolution is thus a scientific fact. But I answer these questions with a hearty "no" and conclude: evolution is therefore *not* a scientific fact. And I shall presently show why I am entitled to say this.

If your teacher is one of those who claim that evolution is a scientific fact, it is easy enough to prove this to be a cock and bull story. But don't try to contradict him in an argumentive manner, for after all, he is the biologist and you are only an ignorant pupil. No, all you have to do is ask him one or two simple questions.

Ask him for example the following, "Sir, can you give me a few examples of evolution that we can see happening today before our eyes?" He will probably name a few examples, but these will all demonstrate that plants and animals can undergo *hereditary changes* (see later), but not that higher organisms can develop from lower organisms, *and only that is evolution.* You stick to your guns and tell your teacher that you are not yet satisfied. You want to see examples of the actual development of lower organisms into higher organisms that can be observed today

15

with your own eyes. Your teacher will probably tell you that this development proceeds so slowly that we cannot see it happening. You persist, and ask him if people have ever seen such a development slowly taking place over the past thousands of years. I hope your teacher's patience will not be exhausted by now, but at least you can draw the conclusion for yourself; nobody has ever seen acutal evolution taking place.

At another occasion, when the opportunity presents itself, you can try out the second question. He asserts that the fossils show that all higher organisms have come from the very lowest ones. Make sure you don't contradict him! Yet, ask him again a few simple questions. Try these for instance, "How do the fossils demonstrate that plants and animals are related to each other and descended from the same primitive organisms?"

"How do fossils demonstrate that the sub-kingdoms ("phyla") of the animal kingdom (e.g. the worms, the molluscs, the coeleterates, the anthropods, the vertebrates) are related to each other?"

"How do the fossils demonstrate that the flowering plants gradually came from the lower plants?"

"How do the fossils demonstrate that the mammals gradually developed from the lower vertebrates?"

Your teacher may give different answers: he may beat around the bush, he may say quite honestly that he does not know, *or* he may also honestly say that those fossil indications do not exist, for that is really the case. Perhaps you may still have the nerve to ask him how he can assert that these points are scientific "facts" when there are absolutely no indications that support these points!

You could also ask him what fossils exist that would indicate that man originated from ape-like an-

cestors. But then there is a chance that he will begin
a long story about Neanderthal man and about a certain fossilized Mr. Pithecanthropus ("ape-man"), because he is most likely not acquainted with the latest
research on this subject. If he does so, he is not aware
that these precious names are no longer significant for
the question of man's descent from ape-like mammals. It is also possible that he has heard of the latest
discoveries of Dr. Richard Leakey in Africa. In 1973
Leakey, although he is an evolutionist himself, had
to admit that his own discoveries of fossilized human
bones rendered with a single stroke all existing theories of man's origin totally worthless; yet he had no
other theory to offer in their stead.

Chapter Three

Everyone Must Beleive

Many biologists are of course well aware of the things I have mentioned. These things are not a mere figment of the imagination of some creationists. Staunch evolutionists have often raised a note of warning; they have pointed to the various vague and unproven tenets of the evolution theory, and to the many facts that are in conflict with it. Note that I refer to careful and critical scientists who know the facts! I know of one professor, an evolutionist, who regularly questioned his students to determine what they actually knew about the evidences in favor of evolution, and especially whether they had a complete picture of all the facts that contradict evolution! I wish that more biology teachers taught their pupils in such an evenly balanced and critical manner about evolution (if indeed they must teach it at all).

But how can we explain that even the specialists, who are well acquainted with the unproven theories and the evidences against evolution continue nonetheless to be confirmed evolutionists? Because they *have* to be! The historians may quarrel about whether the Trojan war did or did not take place, but even if there was never such a war it wouldn't matter very much. But with evolution it is a different case. Suppose there has never been any evolution, what then? *Then all the scientists will have to believe that heaven and earth, plants, animals and men were created by God!* That, most of them flatly refuse to do. They would rather believe in evolution even if there are few or absolutely no proofs of it, and in spite of the many facts that contradict that belief. They plainly are compelled to believe in evolution; they have no choice; they *must* believe.

Wait a minute! Perhaps you are all set to raise your voice in protest. It is very likely that you learned at school that:

> Belief in *evolution* is based on the results of modern scientific research, and it is therefore "scientific."

> Belief in creation is a religious belief, derived from old religious books, and it is therefore "unscientific."

This sounds quite plausible. This sort of assertion has indeed caused an enormous amount of harm, but it is absolutely and completely untrue. I must now point out a few verifiable facts which you must never forget.

1. The evolution doctrine is not at all modern. It is almost as old as mankind. It was generally accepted by the Egyptians, the Babylonians, the Greeks and the Romans. Later this primitive pagan belief was for a long time suppressed by the rise of Christianity. But when, in the last century, there arose everywhere a great resistance to the Christian faith, this pagan superstition was brought from the attic and arrayed in a modern garb.

2.   Darwin's belief in evolution did not result from his explorations: he believed it quite firmly before he began his enormous investigations. And he carried out these explorations chiefly to combat belief in creation. Moreover, today, no one believes in the theory as he propounded it, so you can hardly maintain that his belief in evolution was justified by his (inaccurate) theory. Besides that, you can say that his belief in evolution was easier to justify than today's belief, for in his day the many facts that are in conflict with evolution were not yet known. Now we know that the many predictions that were made on the basis of the theory have not come to pass.

3.   Futhermore, when you read the present day writings of the evolutionists, you see that their belief in evolution is not based upon scientific results, but upon philosophical and humanistic propositions. Some acknowledge quite honestly that, even if all evolutionary theories (which ought to explain the evolutionary process) are shown to be wrong, they would still continue to believe in evolution. This shows that this belief is not "scientific," but founded upon a particular outlook on life. Various evolutionists acknowledge openly that they believe in evolution simply because they reject creation. I know of a book by a certain Professor More which enumerates many and great objections to the theories of evolution, each objection more devastating than the previous one, but at the end he says that he still believes in evolution because he has such a deep aversion to the only other possibility: creation by God!

4.   It is, therefore, first rate nonsense to say that belief in evolution is more scientific than belief

in creation. They are both just as "old fashioned." They are both equally based upon a particular outlook on life. Fundamentally, the difference is this: *belief in creation is based on belief in God and the Bible, belief in evolution is
based on an aversion to belief in God and the
Bible.*

So, what is the truth — Creation or Evolution?

That depends on another question: "Do you believe that the Bible is the inspired, infallible Word of
God?" If you don't, you reject the fact of creation as
God has revealed it to us, and you have nothing left
but the primitive, pagan belief in evolution. In either
case you must *believe* — you cannot leave that to religious people only. You either believe the one, or
you must of necessity believe the other!

Chapter Four

Wiggling Leaves

First of all then you must get this clear: belief in creation and belief in evolution may be considered equally scientific or unscientific, depending on your point of view. If you have understood this, the next question arises: "Which of these two convictions correlates better with the actual facts already known?" Don't expect, however, that anybody on earth could, even after a quiet and unprejudiced review of all the facts, make a well-considered choice between either of these beliefs. We are not unprejudiced, for we either believe in the Bible as the inspired Word of God and therefore in creation, or we reject the Bible and believe in evolution.

Yet, I am prepared to assert that the actual, acknowledged facts better fit the creation doctrine than the evolution doctrine. I say this with full conviction, although most biologists sincerely believe that the facts support the idea of evolution. It is absurd that creationists and evolutionists have exactly the same facts at their disposal and, in spite of this, each group considers those facts to support his own point of view. Nevertheless, that is possible: we can get so entangled in a particular thought pattern that we no longer see the facts that contradict it.

Let me give an example related to me by Dr. Donald Chittick, an American creationist. Dr. Chittick explained that occasionally, he asks his pupils, "Do you know how the wind is produced?" "Of course," one of them will answer, "wind is caused by air flowing from a place with high pressure to a place with low pressure." "Oh no," says Chittick, "you are way behind the times; that is old fashioned theory. We have now discovered that the branches and leaves of the trees move, and through that movement a current of air is produced, and that is the wind. Try to disprove this new theory!"

The pupils are puzzled. A smart one says, "Wind is found in places without trees." But Chittick answers, "That is ingenious, but it won't do, for the wind comes from somewhere where there are trees with wiggling leaves!" Occasionally there is a youngster who knows a good way to disprove this statement. But then Chittick crushes him with his trump card and says, "Boy, the only reason for your old-fashioned talk is that you lack knowledge of the latest developments. Don't you know that men have been on the moon? Well they have discovered that there is no wind on the moon. And why? Because there are no trees with wiggling leaves on the moon!"

But then Chittick becomes serious and says, "Look, that is exactly what the evolutionists do. They have a theory that can be supported by a wealth of facts, but that does not prove at all that it is a sound theory, for all those facts support just as well the opposite "theory," namely, belief in creation. And don't allow yourself to be floored by the so-called latest discoveries that support belief in evolution, for such support does not prove anything."

Chittick is quite right! For example, it is a fact that there is a wonderful pattern running through the entire flora and fauna; so wonderful that you can subdivide the flora and fauna very nicely and naturally in phyla, classes, orders, families, and so on. "Look," says the evolutionist triumphantly, "that is exactly in agreement with my point of view. If all organisms have common ancestors, then I should, even today, be able to recognize their relationship in construction and manner of life." Well, the man is right. All facts agree magnificently with his theory. But this does not prove that he is right, for these relationships are also in perfect agreement with the creationist's viewpoint, with the Biblical image of an orderly God Who created the world according to a perfect and harmonious plan! The facts agree with both viewpoints, and so we are not any closer to answering the question.

Who is right then? Is the one explanation more "scientific" than the other? To maintain this, would be nonsense. The one explanation is more *attractive* than the other; not on scientific grounds, but only depending on the basis of the individual's outlook upon life. Yet there is a difference in the scientific *value* of these two explanations. The idea of evolution would lead one to expect *many* more intermediate forms between the different plants and animals so that the various groups of plants and animals wouldn't be as sharply divided from each other as they generally are. Neither should we have come across so many striking, structural similarities among various groups of organisms, although they are, on other grounds, regarded as only very distantly related. For example, vertebrates and octopuses have remarkably similar eyes; an incredible mystery to the evolutionist who regards these two groups to be very far removed from each other. For the creationist, however, this is no problem. He understands that God would give animals living in similar conditions certain strong resemblances in structure (suited to their circumstances), while those animals would perhaps be very different in other aspects.

This is just one example. For other examples you can refer to a more detailed book. (See list at the back). What I am trying to get across is this: don't be put off by the statement that innumerable observations in nature agree with the doctrine of evolution. That does not mean a thing as long as you have not inquired whether the same observations agree exactly (and perhaps even more so) with the creation doctrine. On the basis of scientific arguments I personally believe the facts agree better with the creation doctrine.

As far as that is concerned, evolutionism is one great house of cards. The biologist, the geologist, or any specialist for that matter, usually knows pretty well where his own profession shows up weaknesses in the evolution doctrine (and many acknowledge these), but he is not too concerned about them, for he thinks, "The proofs provided by my colleagues in the other departments are strong enough." If all think that, you get a delightful soap bubble. Refute the arguments of one profession and they will hide behind the arguments of other professions. Chop off one of the tentacles of the evolution-monster and you are strangled by the other tentacles. Introduce as many scientific objections as you will and they will contrive ingenious "auxiliary theories" to "explain" all the facts that contradict the theory or to reason the objections out of existence, or they simply ignore them! The only sensible thing to do is to attack evolutionism on all fronts at once with an army of creationists. But even that is not good enough because the evolutionists have told us beforehand that, even if we torpedo all their theories, they will still prefer the evolution to the creation doctrine. Their aversion to the creation doctrine is so great that they prefer the theory of "wiggling leaves" anytime.

Chapter Five

Bitter Pills

If the concept of evolution holds true, then the evolutionists must make it acceptable to us on the basis of scientific arguments. They will have to clear up two points for us:

1 Is there a known biological "mechanism" whereby lower, simpler organisms can gradually develop into higher, more complicated organisms? Such a mechanism would particularly belong to the field of *genetics* (the study of heredity).

2 Do the fossils actually give us a picture of a gradual development over millions of years from lower to higher organisms? Such a study of fossils belongs to the field of Paleontology (the study of fossilized organisms).

In the last century these questions were approached with a spirit of optimism. It was thought that the answers to them would soon be found. Well, we have those answers now, and both are a very definite "No!" I must prove this, of course, no matter how bitter these pills may be for the honest, expert evolutionist.

MUTATION = CHANGE WITHIN A POPULATION

Today we know all sorts of principles by which a particular "population" (group, collection) of, for example, a certain animal species can gradually undergo a number of hereditary changes during successive generations. The hereditary factors of living organisms are mainly found in the so-called *genes*. These are infinitesimal structures found in the nuclei of body cells and reproductive cells. Through all sorts of influences from without, arbitrary genes can undergo all sorts of arbitrary changes (mutations). As a result of this the genes begin to act differently, and nearly always less efficiently, or they even cease to act altogether. Organisms with such genes are, therefore, frequently less able to hold their own; they die prematurely or are unable to reproduce themselves satisfactorily.

The evolutionists claim that evolution takes place because once in a while mutations occur which, in certain surroundings *are* favorable, providing the organism with better possibilities for self-preservation. True enough, that does indeed happen once in a while. Under changed conditions of habitat a particular mutation may sometimes turn out to be more favorable. Then we see that the organisms that do not have that particular mutation, gradually disappear from the population. But this is extremely rare, and even then it is usually only of a temporary nature. Generally it happens because *man* has made a drastic change in the environment. Moreover, this only demonstrates that populations can experience certain "oscillations," but this has absolutely (and I mean *absolutely*) nothing to do with our question of how higher organisms (that is, with a more complicated, more perfect construction) can develop from lower organisms! The experts in genetics have long been convinced that the "genetic mechanisms" in living organisms do not strive to change the population, but rather to keep it as balanced and constant as possible. *Within* such a population it is possible that, under the influence of environmental changes, all sorts of variations appear, but this is quite another thing from the whole population developing to a higher rung on the evolutionary ladder.

You'd better make sure that you understand this well, for there is a great deal of deception in this field. By far the majority of the biological "proofs" of evolution that are presented in the textbooks have to do with such changes *within* the population. At times we call this micro-evolution, but that is misleading because it has nothing to do with evolution! It is simply variation, change, oscillation, not ascent. All those jubilant proofs of micro-evolution have nothing to do with our question, "How on earth could *macro*-evolution ever have taken place?" Or, "How could mammals originate from reptiles; amphibians from fish, and so forth?" Everything we know about genetics makes it highly improbable that such developments are even remotely possible.

Let me give you an example of this sort of deception. If you go to the American Museum of Natural History in New York, you will find among other things, that a whole series of fossilized horses is portrayed. Supposedly these horses gradually developed from each other over a period of hundreds of thousands of years. The series begins with a small animal that has, quite conventionally, five toes on each foot. Each of the following animals is a little larger and the number of toes gradually decreases until finally only the middle toe remains, and that is the well known horse's hoof. Wouldn't you say that this is a wonderful proof of evolution? You would almost think so, for this "story of the horse" is one of the most popular arguments in favor of evolution.

But what is the truth of the matter? Suppose the series is genuine: the last horses in the series have indeed developed from the first in the series. Would we then have a proof of evolution? Certainly not: they are still horses, aren't they? The series demonstrates that many variations are possible on the theme "horse," but it does not show that higher organisms can develop from lower organisms. Take a look at the toes. You are more likely to see *degeneration* than evolution. But what is worse: there is not a single proof that these horses have developed in the order in which they are displayed! Besides, there are indications that in the time of the first (i.e., the "oldest") animal in the series, modern looking horses were in existence. If that is true, we may as well pack up. These horse-fossils come from different parts of the world (could those horses really have developed from each other?) and from places of which the relative age is absolutely uncertain.

Isn't it outrageous that such things are shown to the general public who are thereby fooled into thinking that evolution is a fact? Unfortunately there is no shortage of such poppy cock in museums and popular books. What do you think of the pretty pictures, portraying prehistoric people as wild monsters with ape-like appearances? Pure deceit! It is totally impossible to establish from the evidence of skulls and bones what anyone's face, hair, color of skin, etc. would have looked like. For a long time the Neanderthal man was hailed as one of the most important missing links between apes and men. In pictures he is presented as a wild looking ape-man. But little by little scientists have come to the conclusion that if we were to meet a Neanderthal man in a supermarket, he would not at all be conspicuous! Let us hope your teacher knows this, and that he does not persist in dishing up "old hat."

THE FOSSILS

This naturally leads us to the next question, "What have the fossils to say to us?" You will understand of course, that I can cover these points only in a brief and superficial manner. That doesn't matter very much, for at school they tell you that evolution is a fact, and then the so-called "evidences" for it are only very briefly and superficially referred to. I would be satisfied if you learned to see that things could well be different from what most biology and religious teachers claim they are.

You know that the earth's crust consists of a large number of layers, called "strata." These are formed either because fluid rock came out of the earth (for example, out of volcanoes) and solidified; or because the wind carried grains of sand and clay and deposited them somewhere; or glaciers forced up sand or clay; or, more frequently, sand, clay, limestone, etc., settled out in seas, lakes, and rivers. In the latter types of strata we come across innumerable petrified remains of plants and animals that once lived on the earth. Especially the harder elements, such as shells, scales and bones were easily fossilized.

Normally the lower strata are (of course) older and the upper strata younger. The claim of evolutionists is as follows: in the lower (therefore the older) strata we find the simpler fossilized organisms, and when we come to the higher (and therefore the younger) strata, we find, beside the lower, also higher and more complicated fossilized organisms. All the strata containing fossils span a period of about 600 million years (so they assert), and in that period we see how the history of life began with very simple organisms, and how, in the course of the ages, progressively higher organisms appear.

Marvellous, isn't it? Isn't that the most beautiful proof of evolution? Certainly . . . if the story were true, that is! This is what they usually tell you, but just the same, *it is very deceitful*! It might as well be admitted that there is not a trace of truth in the whole story. Nowhere in the whole world do you find all those strata one above the other in such a fashion that the lower organisms are found at the bottom and both the lower and higher ones at the top. Besides, not just simple organisms are found in the fossil-containing strata that are considered to be the oldest, but it has been discovered that nearly *all* the phyla of the fauna are represented in them. The vertebrates form the only exception to this, but they appear *immediately* in the next layers, *without any intermediate forms*!

Where do all these different groups of animals come from? Where are the common ancestors that, according to the theory, they must have had? If the theory is right, then three-quarters, and according to some, even nine-tenths, of the history of life is missing! How is it that there are hardly any fossils from this enormous period? Could it be that the common ancestors never existed?

I suppose you expect that the oldest strata must always lie at the bottom. But that is not so at all! The order of the strata can be totally disturbed; layers with fossils of higher organisms may be underneath, while layers with exclusively simple organisms may lie on the top. In a few instances you can plainly see that the layers have been turned upside down by a kind of earthquake, but frequently every trace of such enormous disturbances of the earth's crust is lacking. So in all fairness you would have to conclude that the layers were apparently formed in the order in which they are found. How dare the evolutionistic geologists simply claim that the strata are upside down, in spite of all this?

Yes, that is a painful story. How does the evolutionist determine the age of a strata? He can not see it from the material of which it is made. The *order* of the layers obviously does not help him much either, for the so-called "youngest" layers may be underneath and the so-called "oldest" layers may be on top. Perhaps you expect that he has some special methods of measuring the age (you may have heard of radioactive dating methods, of which more later). Wrong again: for this type of layer such dating methods cannot help him. How then can he see if one layer is older or younger than another? You would never guess: *he can tell by the fossils contained in them*! Especially the so-called "index-fossils," which are not so common, are characteristic (so they tell us) of a particular geological "period."

Isn't that delightful? When simple fossils (those of lower organisms) appear in a layer, then that is an old layer, and when there are complicated fossils (of higher organisms) in a layer, than that is a young layer. This may be expressing it a little too simply, but that is really the gist of the matter. Even in learned geological articles this enormous "circular reasoning" has been acknowledged. It goes like this: "How can you prove that the higher organisms are younger than the lower ones?" Answer: "Because the former are found in the younger strata." Question: "But how do you know which strata are younger and which are older?" Answer: "You can see that by the fossils found in them, higher organisms are found in younger layers." Question: "But how can you prove that the higher organisms are younger than the lower organisms?" Answer: "Because the former are found in younger strata than the latter." Question: "But how do you know which strata . . . . ?"

. . . Oh, I give up, for you have already noticed that we are running around in circles. And that, you see, is considered the evidence of the fossils!

There are, besides, innumerable other problems that are insurmountable, connected with the evidence of the fossils. Don't forget that *if* the simple organisms were indeed the first to appear, and only after millions of years the higher organisms (a supposition which we have seen to be highly debatable), this would by itself, still not be a *proof* that the higher ones developed from the lower. In order to make this plausible the geologists would have to come forward with thousands of intermediary and transitional forms between the various groups of animals and between the various groups of plants.

A hundred years ago scientists were very optimistic that those "missing links" would be found, but famous evolutionists are beginning to acknowledge openly that perhaps those "missing links" never existed. The (unbridgeable) gaps between the various groups were in the past just as wide as they are today, however bitter to swallow that pill may be for the evolutionists.

Do the fossils indicate evolution? Perhaps . . . but then only to those who already have an unshakable faith in evolution. More sober people know better.

Chapter Six

Dripping Taps

When we talk of strata and fossils, however, there must be at least one other point bothering you — the juggling with millions and billions of years.

Your teacher, brazen faced, may tell you, *"This layer is so many millions of years old, and that fossil so many thousands."* How does he know this? He has learned it from the writings of the evolutionists. And where did they get it from? Well, in the past the evolutionists just invented all those figures. They simply needed those millions of years to support their claim that by means of extremely gradual modifications all higher organisms descended from the simpler. True, as time went by, well-known mathematicians demonstrated that even a million times a million years would still not suffice for such a descent, but never mind.

But then the radioactive dating methods came along, and suddenly "proof" of those millions of years was available. In essence, these methods are based on quantitative measurements of substances that are converted or formed by so-called "radioactive processes," and the measurement of the speed at which these substances originate. Let me give you an example that explains how all these measurements work in principle.

Just imagine that I have a very large tank with a dripping tap over it. I start measuring, and discover that a gallon of water drips out of the tap in one hour and that there are exactly one hundred gallons of water in the tank. Question: "How long has the tap been leaking?" That is not difficult, you might say. There are one hundred gallons, each hour a gallon is added, so the tap has been dripping for one hundred hours. Wrong! The tap has been leaking for only ten hours! You didn't know that a lot of water was already in the tank before the tap started to drip, then someone poured a few buckets of water in as well, and thirdly in the beginning the tap was dripping much faster than it is now. You could not know all this of course, but you *should* have known that you ought to have answered, "The tap has been leaking one hundred hours, *provided* that the tank was initially empty *and* that no one interfered with the tap and the tank, and that the tap has been dripping at a constant rate."

Here you have the mistake the evolutionists are making. They pretend to be able to measure the age of strata and fossils, but in fact they only measure quantities of matter and rates of conversion. To deduce the age from this information, you must be certain about several things. First of all, what were the original quantities of the different materials at the moment the rock or fossils were formed ; secondly, that external factors have not influenced the process; and thirdly, that the rate of conversion has always remained the same. The enormous difficulty is that we can not speak with certainty about any one of these three points. If we are not sure of even *one* of these three points, we simply cannot make any definite statement about the ages of rocks.

Usually the evolutionists answer this by saying, "Yes, but when we use entirely different methods and still get the same results, then we are sure that we have established the correct age." Certainly, but how often have they obtained such agreement? There is a well-known human skull of a distant "ancestor" of ours, who bears the charming name of Zinjanthropus. By a certain method it has been "established" that this skull is 1¾ million years old. But Dr. R. L. Whitelaw has recently applied the radio-carbon method to the same skull and found its age to be 10,000 years! Quite a big difference, don't you think so?

But things are getting even better! During the last few years the radio active dating method has been applied to volcanic rocks which were known to have been formed only 100 or 200 years ago during volcanic eruptions. Unsuspecting scientists were asked to determine the "age" of those rocks, and what did they discover? You have guessed it: millions and millions of years. And this happened not once, but many times, with stone from all over the world. Could it be that something is wrong with the highly praised dating methods and with the entire geological timescale?

I have already said that it is nonsense to assert that belief in evolution is more "scientific" than belief in creation. If one of these two *would* be more scientific than the other it could be ascertained in only one way. That is: when you begin a particular research project you must dare, on the basis of your conviction or the theory, to make solid predictions as to what you expect to find. If those predictions do not materialize then your theory is "on the rocks" or at least is badly damaged. Well, that is just what has happened at the time of the first moon flights! The evolutionists maintained that the moon was billions of years old, and throughout all those years meteorites had been crashing upon it. Because the moon has no atmosphere, meteorites do not pulverize or burn up before they crash on the moon's surface. So there had to be a thick layer of dust on the moon which, taking the tremendous age of the moon into account, should be half a dozen feet thick. Therefore, the landing craft were provided with special, expensive bearing pads. "Fellows," the creationists said, "you can save yourselves all that money, for the moon is at the most 10,000* years old and there will hardly be an inch of dust there!" Well, that was a solid prediction, was it not? For once we could see who is right. Well, you know the answer. When the first men walked around on the moon they were forced to acknowledge that, to their surprise, there was hardly an inch of dust lying on the moon.

That is just one example. Can you understand why some people find creationism more acceptable than evolutionism? A professor of Physics at the University of Texas, Th. Barnes, is one such person. Recently I had lunch with him, and he told me about his study of earth magnetism. You know that the earth has a magnetic field which causes the compass needles always to point to the North. But do you know that these magnetic forces are very slowly becoming weaker? Professor Barnes has measured this weakening process very accurately and has calculated that the earth can at the most be 10,000 years old. If the earth were much older, its magnetism must once have been so strong, that the earth would have burst apart by its own magnetic powers.

*Of course, for the same reasons that dating methods which indicate millions of years, methods which indicate very short periods of time may also be in error. We simply cannot know with accuracy the age of the earth, nor is it really important for one who believes the Word of God as to creation.

This sort of problem is never made known to the general public. John Q. Public must get the idea that all is well with the theory of evolution. The facts are suppressed. What do you think of this, for example. The evolutionists assert that the dinosaurs (you know, those enormous, prehistoric monsters) were extinct for 70 million years before man came on the scene. But suppose we discovered strata with petrified footprints of both dinosaurs and men, what then? Suppose those footprints were even overlaying each other so that we couldn't doubt that they originated at the same time? Would we not be forced to conclude that men and dinosaurs lived at the same time?

Well, that is exactly what has been found in cretaceous rocks on the banks of the Paluxy River near the village of Glen Rose in Texas! Clever geologists have carefully studied those footprints by special methods to make sure that they really came from dinosaurs and men, and that they were not carvings. But do you realize what this discovery (and it is only one out of many) means? "If it is really true," one geologist wrote, "that man and dinosaurs lived at the same time, then the entire historical geology collapses and the geologists may as well become truck drivers!"

So, what do evolutionistic geologists do? Either they get very angry and cry, "Deceit, lies!"; or they resort to learned dissertations which no one understands but which are supposed to show that they are right anyway; or else they just shrug their shoulders in a superior fashion and simply ignore the whole matter.

Chapter Seven

Old Hat

Now let us hope that your biology teacher has kept abreast of the times and has remained up to date in his own field; and let us hope that those who give you religious instruction have read more than only sensational and popular booklets about evolution. Otherwise it is more than likely that, with the best intentions, your teachers will dish up all kinds of "old hat" that has long ago been rejected by the specialists.

Does your teacher still tell you that the Neanderthal man and Pithecanthropus (the ape man from Java) were intermediate forms between apes and men? That's all old hat. It is now generally accepted that these two gentlemen were ordinary men, even if they might have looked a bit strange — but not any stranger than some specimens that walk around among us. Moreover, we know that people who looked just like us lived before these prehistoric people!

Does your teacher still tell you the old story that the embryonic development of man (i.e. his development before birth) is a kind of recapitulation of his evolutionary history? It's all old hat, refuted long ago.

Does your teacher still tell you, for instance, that unborn people, at a certain early stage, have gill slits and a tail which prove that we have evolved from animals with gill slits and tails? Nothing but old hat. They are not even gill slits, but very necessary and important grooves from which all kinds of organs arise. Besides, as I told you already, *correspondence* can never be proof of *descent*.

Does your teacher still tell you that man has several degenerated organs that no longer have a function; organs that supposedly are remainders of distant animal ancestors that could use them? That's what people believed at one time because the function of many organs (such as the appendix, the thymus, the tailbone) were still unknown. But today we know these functions much better and we know that the thymus, for instance, is a most important organ!

Does your teacher still tell you that it is only a matter of years before scientists will produce a living cell? It is all old hat. People used to think that way when they assumed that cells were simply drops of water with certain substances in them. With the passing of time we acquired some knowledge of the incredible complicated structure of a single living cell. Mathematicians have calculated that trillions of years wouldn't suffice to make it even conceivable that something so intensely beautiful could be produced by what is, in fact, pure chance. For a living cell to come from lifeless matter would be an even greater miracle than the descent of man from that single cell! Don't let them fool you with tales of modern (and actually fantastic) experiments and discoveries. The results so far achieved are rather like those of someone who, with a great deal of trouble, has at last managed to manufacture a brick and now thinks that it will be no problem at all to build a cathedral. After all, suppose that hundreds of clever men, with the help of the most modern and most expensive apparatus, managed to construct a living cell: what would that prove? Certainly not that life could have ever originated by itself, by pure chance, out of dead matter; it would rather indicate that life could only have originated by means of a highly intelligent and powerful mind — *that of God Himself!*

Chapter Eight

Biblical Answers

It is quite natural that you begin to wonder what is the truth about those fossils and strata. How do the creationists (those people that believe in creation) suppose the strata came into existence if there is no reason to assume that they originated in the course of millions of years?

That is a good question! It is one thing for the creationists to say that the evolutionists are all wrong, but let them come forward with a better explanation. Well that is just what they do! They present a better explanation, based on the Bible, but at the same time it is scientifically justifiable. The Bible itself is plainly not a textbook of science, but that does not mean (as some people foolishly and naively conclude) that the Bible is therefore unreliable when it comes, for instance, to origins. What God says in His Word is true, even if it is not formulated in our western, twentieth-century manner of speech.

For example, the Bible says on the first page that God created the plants and the animals "after their kind." At first sight it may not be clear what this expression means, but in the original language of the Bible it means: God created them "in their variety of forms." God did not create by means of an evolutionary process, but He created at the same time a number of "forms" side by side. The biologists may determine how wide this concept of "form" is. At any rate it is in most instances wider than the concept of "species" that biologists refer to. The "dog" is a biological species within which innumerable breeds can be distinguished, but dogs can also be crossbred with the species of "wolf." But the group is not much wider; dogs and wolves cannot be crossbred with other related species. God has created a large number of forms which are plainly and sharply distinguished from each other because they show great external differences and cannot be crossbred with each other. That is exactly what biology has established. Within one such "form" organisms may vary endlessly; breeders and nurserymen may give a helping hand by directed crossbreeding, but they are not able to violate the bounds which God has imposed upon these groups.

In this little booklet I do not want to write too much of what Genesis 1 and 2 have to say about creation. Here I am only concerned with the question, What should you believe: creation or evolution? And now that we have seen that we have no choice but to believe that God created everything, I would just like to draw attention to three great Biblical facts. These facts will help you a little in understanding nature as we see it around us. First, I have just stated that the Bible teaches us that God created a number of distinct animal and plant forms, and the bounds that exist between those forms can be observed anywhere in nature.

The second great fact is not found in the creation story, but in Genesis 3; it is the story of man's fall.

You know that Adam and Eve, the first human couple, were, alas, disobedient to God and fell into sin. That fall had disastrous results, not just for themselves, but also for the entire creation. Decay and destruction made their appearance everywhere. The Apostle Paul puts it this way, "For the creature has been made subject to vanity, . . . the whole creation groans together and travails in pain together until now" (Romans 8:20, 22). You can see this everywhere around you. The universe is just like a huge alarm clock, wound up and running down slowly. Men and animals (if they don't die in an accident) die an irrevocable, natural death and their bodies decay. The stars in the sky (even our sun) are slowly but surely burning up, just as candles. One of the basic laws in physics expresses this more or less as follows: Everywhere in nature we observe the tendency for *order* to give gradually way to *disorder.* Man (and God) can bring a certain order in a particular situation, but when things are left to themselves they fade, perish, rot away and are consumed. Everyone who studies nature discovers the great truth of this law. But what do the evolutionists say? They claim that during billions of years an evolution has taken place whereby ever *increasing* "order," ever more complex and higher forms arose out of a condition of "disorder." Scientifically this is pure nonsense. It just cannot be, and there is not a biologist who has been able to squirm out of this insurmountable problem. The Bible, however, is clear enough. The world was created good and perfect, but since the fall of man it is under the dominion of death, decay and destruction. There is no evolution (progress), but degeneration (regression).

The Bible teaches us a third thing that is of great importance for our subject. In the book of Genesis chapters 6 to 8, we read that at one time the human race, even the entire earth, was destroyed by the

Flood. That was not just another flood! Just read the whole account and you will see that, for instance, the whole crust of the earth broke open so that the entire surface of the earth was churned up. If you believe God at His Word and you see that He once destroyed the earth at such a great scale, then you should ask some geologist what the consequences would be of a flood similar to the one described in the Bible.

Creationistic geologists and physicists have written many books on this subject. In these books they point out that such a deluge, in which the whole of the earth's surface was churned up, must also have been accompanied by mighty tidal waves and the forming of ice caps. In such a flood the churned up materials that would slowly settle out would be mixed with the remains of dead organisms, especially of the simpler ones that would be least able to resist the current.

How simply does this solve the problems! Now we understand how the so-called"oldest" fossil-bearing strata, that are full of fossils representing nearly *all* the phyla of the animal kingdom, can be found right on top of a bottom layer that is totally devoid of fossils.

Now we can also understand why we normally come across the higher animals, which can swim quite well, in the higher layers, and the land animals normally in higher layers yet. The exceptions of this rule (including the apparent overturning of strata to which we referred) are now much easier understood than if evolution had taken place.

Now that we are beginning to be knowledgeable about the Flood, we can more readily understand why there are so many fossils. Under normal conditions fossils are not formed at all; they originate especially well in running water where they are quickly covered by solid materials — exactly as we would expect with a severe flood!

Now we can also understand why, in so many places on the earth, colossal mass-graves have been discovered containing hundreds of thousands of fossilized animals heaped together. These animals fled in mortal fear from the rising waters and were finally overtaken by them.

Now we understand as well why so many mammoths are found in the ice of Siberia. They were so suddenly overtaken by the freezing waters that some had their food still in their mouths, and their flesh hasn't even decayed.

In principle the evolutionists and the creationists think alike on the formation of the strata — it is just that the former believe that millions of years were required for the process, while the latter believe that most of them came into being in a few years, that is, the layers were quickly placed one on top of the other by mighty tidal movements, but after that it took of course some years before they were petrified. It is very important to be aware of the repeated assertions of creationistic geologists. Again and again they stress the point that, when the layers were deposited on top of each other, the lower layers could not possibly have been petrified as yet. The evolutionists say they must have been petrified. In their line of thought, since a stratum formed on top of another one millions of years after the former stratum had been formed, naturally the former stratum must have been petrified long before. But the creationists point out, for example, that fossilized tree trunks have been found which reach through a number of strata. That proves unmistakably that those layers were formed shortly after each other, when not one of them was petrified.

Another example is the famous Grand Canyon in the United States which splendidly displays all the layers on top of each other because the winding Colorado River has carved deep ravines in them. Everywhere plaques are placed telling the tourist how many millions of years apart, the formation of the different strata took place. But that is really impossible! Just look what the river has done. It has carved deep ravines downwards as it meandered (describing many curves), so it has eroded the banks sidewards. According to physics the river could only do both things simultaneously if the strata were soft when the erosion took place. During the Flood these soft layers were quickly piled on top of each other, and shortly after, the river carved its way through them; only much later the strata were gradually petrified.

Don't let them tell you that millions of years were required for the formation of minerals (coal, oil) although this is often said to be the case. In laboratories men have copied their formation artificially, and we know now that in a few days or even hours minerals can be formed that, according to earlier beliefs, would have taken millions of years to form. In such a small booklet I cannot, of course, mention all the books and articles in which all these things are to be found (although your teacher may think, if he reads this, that these are only my individual thoughts). I do not feel compelled to give such an enumeration, for the majority of textbooks and teachers are satisfied with a considerable smaller number of "proofs" for evolution than the number of counterproofs that I have given here. Nevertheless, at the back of this booklet there is a short list of books and brochures that can give you further help.

Chapter Nine

Now What ?

Now you have seen what the situation is. There are people who in advance believe in evolution (often because they detest the thought of creation), so they fit the scientific facts into that belief. There are also people who believe God and His Word and who make room for the facts in *that* belief. You have also seen that these latter people are more successful in their attempt than the former. They stick to the facts and give a better explanation of them. The explanation of the evolutionists rattles on every side, but they are deaf to this! In the ordinary course of science you can always replace one theory with a better one. But the evolutionists can't do that: no matter how many facts contradict their theory they have no choice but to "explain them away" or to neglect them. The doctrine itself can never disappear, for there is nothing to take its place — except, of course, belief in the God Who created all things, but that they do not want!

And *you*, what are *you* going to do? Do you intend to study, without prejudice, as many facts as you can, to read as many books of evolutionists *and* creationists as you can, so that you can select eventually the more scientific explanation?

Forget it! In the end you will choose either for creation or for evolution, not on the basis of any scientific arguments, but on the basis of faith. When it comes to one's view of scientific explanations, no one can make an unprejudiced choice out of various scientific explanations. He will say, "I find the scientific arguments of the creationists (or evolutionists) better" — why? Because he *believes* in creation (or evolution)!

At one time it was supposed that scientists could provide themselves with all the facts, study them and thus arrive at scientific theories without the least of prejudice. But experience has proven that this is not so. If creationists were to say such a thing, they wouldn't be believed, but one of the greatest philosophers now living, Karl Popper, has said the same thing. For decades he has emphasized that we do not collect the facts without prejudice at all. We collect those facts that concern and support the particular notions we have already in our minds, and we interpret them, as much as possible, in accordance with these notions. Popper has also driven the point home that new facts that agree with a particular theory, or that could be made to agree with it (as the evolutionists always do), do not prove at all that the theory is right. The very same facts may just as well agree with an entirely opposing theory (such as in this case, creationism).

Initially, people thought that Popper was off his rocker, but now most people see that he is right. The man deserves a statue; the English have already given him knighthood. Bear this in mind: evolutionists are not more objective or more scientific than creationists. Both begin with *faith*! Don't tell me, you thought that by unprejudiced research you could determine how the world came into being. Not at all! "Through *faith* we understand that the worlds were framed by the Word of God, so that things which are seen were not made of things which do appear" (Hebrews 11:3).

What kind of faith is it of which Hebrews 11 speaks? Is it somewhat like, "Well, I don't know for sure, but I *believe* it"? Certainly not! This faith is a faith through which people subdued kingdoms, wrought righteousness, obtained promises, stopped the mouths of lions, quenched the violence of fire" (verses 33 and 34). That is *some faith*! "Science" is not real knowledge; it can only say, "It must *presumably* have happened in this way." But the Bible's faith does not speak that way. It says, "Faith is the substance of things hoped for, the evidence of things not seen" (Hebrews 11:1).

How is that possible? Because this faith does not rest on human reasonings, but on the revealed Word of God. Was there anyone present when the world came into being? *God* was there, and the Creator of the world is the Author of the Bible. And the Bible says a lot more about faith. "Without faith it is impossible to please Him, for he that comes to God must believe that He is, and that He is a Rewarder of them that diligently seek Him" (Hebrews 11:6). Ah, that goes even a step farther! Faith does not only teach us the origin of creation, but faith causes us to know the Creator! Are *you* such an earnest seeker? Are you only looking for truth concerning evolution or creation, or have you already started out on an earnest search for the Creator Himself?

Do you know why it is so difficult to really seek God and find Him? Just listen to what Isaiah says, "Your iniquities have separated between you and your God, and your sins have hid His face from you, that He will not hear" (Isaiah 59:2). Have you asked yourself why so many people believe in evolution? Of course, most of them know no better. But the great champions sometimes confess that it is because they detest the Creator and the Bible. Man is not an earnest seeker of God; he is an enemy of God. He hates God because he knows that, although God is a rewarder of those who seek Him (as we just read), He is also One Who punishes those who hate Him and turn their back on Him, who go their own way. That is what sin is all about: to go your own way, to do your own will, not to bother about God Who is your Creator and (if you don't change) your Judge.

According to the evolutionists, man is a refined animal that has triumphantly climbed from deep down depths to highest heights to climb yet higher still. According to the Bible it is just the other way around. God created man perfect, but by his horrible disobedience, he fell into sin. And from then on, man has not gone up and up, but down and down on a path that will end, not in the highly developed superman, but in eternal judgment, far away from God's grace.

But yet, if there are among these human multitudes some seekers, persons who earnestly seek God, then He is their Rewarder. He Himself draws people, changes their hostile attitude, renews them and redeems them. This little booklet you have in your hand right now is one of the means whereby God is drawing you this very moment. God says, "Seek Me and live" (Amos 5:4). Do you choose the majority which is on its way to everlasting judgment? Remember, the majority is *never* right: even in the history of science this holds true. Don't be misled by numbers. Seekers after God are few, but they receive a reward of which the evolutionist has not the faintest notion!

That reward embraces everything God has to offer you in His Son, Jesus Christ, by Whom He created the world *and* by Whom He can redeem from their sins all who come to Him confessing their sins. When such seekers, fully trusting, lay their hand on the mighty results of the redemptive work that Christ accomplished on the cross of Golgotha, their life will be radically changed. There is no happier life than a life with God, Who will become your Father, and with His Son Jesus Christ Who will become your Savior and Lord if you put your trust in Him.

I sincerely hope that you will not put this booklet down without a firm determination to begin reading the Bible. A Bible can be bought anywhere rather inexpensively. Search therein for God, for His Son. Pray, get down on your knees, and confess to Him that until now, you have turned your back upon Him, that you have been going your own way, (that is, the way of sin), without paying any attention to Him. Simply acknowledge to Him that you need salvation, because otherwise you will be lost forever. And then accept that great gift that God is offering to all who honestly and sincerely come to Him. That gift is His Son. By the Son of God all things were created and everything is subject to Him. But this Son also became Man to suffer and die for all who were lost but would turn and cry to God for salvation. God does not ignore anyone who asks of Him! He receives him and blesses him forever. Wouldn't *you* like to have this as *your* prospect?

Other Books

If you want to know more about Evolution and Creation you may be able to find the following books in your Christian Bookstore.

SCIENTIFIC CREATIONISM
by Henry M. Morris
Creation Life Publishers,
San Diego, CA.

THE CREATION EXPLANATION
by Robert E. Kofahl & Kelly L. Segraves
Harold Shaw Publishers,
Wheaton, Illinois